Money to Spend

by Maggie Fitzgerald
Illustrated by Patricia Keeler

Glenview, Illinois • Boston, Massachusetts • Chandler, Arizona
Upper Saddle River, New Jersey

Ryan O'Brien wanted to earn some money.
He earned a bundle by painting the neighbor's fence.
Ryan O'Brien counted his money.
He had five dollars and fifty-five cents!

Ryan O'Brien sat down on the ground.
He arranged his money once more.
"Five dollars, two quarters, a nickel," he said.
"I think I will go to the store!"

dollar

quarter

nickel

Ryan O'Brien walked to the store.
The store had some books and some toys.
Ryan O'Brien picked out a drum.
He played it. It made a loud noise!

Ryan O'Brien looked at the price.
"This drum is expensive. It costs lots of money."
Ryan O'Brien put the drum back.
He picked up a book. It was funny.

Ryan O'Brien wanted the book.
He had enough money to buy it.
Ryan O'Brien was going to pay.
He saw a plane and wanted to fly it.

Ryan O'Brien thought a long time.
Should he buy the book or the plane?
Ryan O'Brien looked out the window.
He saw it was starting to rain.

Ryan O'Brien put down the plane.
He put the book back on the pile.
Ryan O'Brien bought an umbrella.
He walked home with 55 cents—and
   a smile!